I0170224

# Long Run Hacks: 20 Ultimate Tips to Help You Push Through Hard Runs!

by Scott Oscar Morton

LERK Publishing, LLC
www.lerkpublishing.com

Edited by Megan Zufelt

Cover by LERK Publishing, LLC.

**ISBN** 978-1-947010-18-5

**Follow me on Facebook and Twitter:**

Twitter: @BeginR2FinishR

Facebook: facebook.com/BeginnerToFinisher/

Website: www.halfmarathonforbeginners.com

Email: scottmorton@halfmarathonforbeginners.com

# Long Run Hacks

To my Friend Preston B.
His life was far from long enough.

## **EXTRA Special Thanks to My Launch Team**

### **U.K.**
Dick Bak
Elaine Corstin
Helen H.
Dianne Leih
Antony Moore
Kevin Moseley
Tania O'Connell
Samia Shaikh
John Turney
Anthony Woodward

### **U.S.A.**
Mark Anderson
Louise Friedman
Mieke G.
Emily Goodin
Shari Harwood
Thomas Hostetter
Alma Rouse
Lori Snee
Al Y.

## Medical Disclaimer

The information in this book is meant to supplement, not replace, proper training. A sport involving speed, equipment, balance and environmental factors, and running, will involve some inherent risk. The authors and publisher advise readers to take full responsibility for their safety and know their limits. Before practicing the skills described in this book, be sure that your equipment is well maintained, and do not take risks beyond your level of experience, aptitude, training, and comfort level.

## **<u>Why I Wrote This Book</u>**

Being a new runner myself, one of the toughest aspects of running long distances is the long run. Since I started writing over a year ago, I began receiving emails from my subscribers detailing their long run struggles as new runners. If you've read my other book, *Beginner's Guide to Half Marathons*, you'll know that I openly admitted that I had a total of three lousy runs and still went on to run a total of seven half marathons to date. All runners, especially new runners, will struggle with the long run from time to time.

When you read through this book it's important to remember the reason why there is a weekly long run in every long-distance race training schedule. The main purpose of a two hour plus long-distance run is not necessarily about how far you go but how long you're on your feet running. It's not about speed, unless you are an elite runner. If you need to take a short walk break at the end of each mile of your long-distance run, then do it. It's not cheating and it's perfectly ok as a new runner. All the tips I share within this book I have personally used at least once to help motivate me on my long-distance runs. If you struggle with long runs from time to time, I hope these tips can help you as well.

## **<u>Injuries & Medical Conditions</u>**

If you have sports-related injuries, I highly suggest that you talk to a medical professional to determine if you are fit enough to run. Not seeking medical advice could further exacerbate an existing injury. I am not a legal or medical professional, nor am I offering any legal or medical advice. One last time, if you're injured or have medical conditions that may prevent you from taking on a rigorous running training program, please seek the opinion of a licensed physician before participating in any physical training.

## <u>Assumptions</u>

Before you dive into this book, I'm assuming the following:

- You've been running for at least six months.
- You run at least one long run a week.
- You're seeking motivation to get you through long runs.

## Other Books by Scott Oscar Morton

If you would like to know when I publish my new eBook releases, please **sign up by clicking here**. You can read all these eBooks for **FREE with Kindle Unlimited**. **Click on the book titles below to buy or read with Kindle Unlimited.**

### Beginner to Finisher Series:

### Available Now:

**Book 1:** *Why New Runners Fail: 26 Ultimate Tips You Should Know Before You Start Running!*

**Book 2:** *5K Fury: 10 Proven Steps to Get You to the Finish Line in 9 weeks or less!*

**Book 3:** *10K Titan: Push Beyond the 5K in 6 Weeks or Less!*

**Book 4:** *Beginner's Guide to Half Marathons: A Simple Step-By-Step Solution to Get You to the Finish Line in 12 Weeks!*

**Book 5:** *Long Run Hacks: 20 Ultimate Tips to Help You Push Through Hard Runs!*

### Coming Soon:

**Book 6:** *Marathon Machine - Breakthrough Your Running Barrier and Conquer Your Dream!*

# Long Run Hacks

# Long Run Hacks

## Table of Contents

# Long Run Hacks

# Tip #1

## Change Your Geography

If you run the same location every time you go for a run, try to change things up. Running the same route at the same time does have its benefits. One reason we run the same route every time is for the familiarity and safety of knowing where we are and what might be out of place. For some runners, this is a must, and if you are that type of runner, I won't try to pry you away from your routine. However, science has shown that changing up a routine habit can cause your neural pathways to expand and grow in different directions. For instance, if you normally run in your neighborhood, instead you could find a local park that has a trail that matches the length of run your training demands. If your routine is to run in the park, maybe you can run on a track. If you live by a beach you could run on the sand. If you're lucky enough to live in the mountains, you can participate in trail running.

By changing up the geography, you're changing up your physical and mental state by adding new surroundings and stimuli. Your physical body will also experience the change in location due to the change in the terrain, such as running in sand or running more hills than your used to. By changing up the routine, you're helping your body release from the exact routine which can cause different muscles to work that normally don't get used in your "go to" routine run locations. With the modern smartphone, it's now possible to just start running in any direction with little preparation. When you are done running, you can call someone and give them a way point via your smartphone to come pick you up based on a GPS location. Or you can just have Lyft or Uber pick up for a fee and take you back to your starting location. The one drawback to this type of running is that at the end of running you are usually doused in sweat, and the driver might not appreciate you getting in the car after you ran 10 miles. You can also try running in a circuit or loop back where you run half the distance from your current start point and then when you reach the halfway point you run back to your starting point. I used this technique for all my long runs which led up to my first half marathon race.

If you want to change up the location where you run, you can add an environmental factor in such as running in the rain or snow. I honestly don't suggest running in either but some people, depending on where they reside, have no other choice. I have run both in the rain and snow, and both require more gear such as booties to help keep your feet dry and raincoats or extra layers of clothing to keep the body warm. Sometimes a run in either of these conditions can help you appreciate running in a much more pleasant environment.

## **Action steps:**

- Change up your geography by running in various locations like the beach, neighborhoods, parks, or mountain trails.
- Try running in a loop back by running half the distance to a point and then run the other half back to your starting point.
- When you change your location, you help your muscles work and rebuild in new ways based on the new terrain.

# Long Run Hacks

## Tip #2

### Rediscover the Joy of Running

Have you ever been running and started to wonder why you are bothering? If you have had these thoughts, you're not alone. First let's define running. When I refer to the term within this book, I'm referring to someone who runs with intent. That intent can be anything from training for a race through trying to lose weight to getting in shape for the long term. When you're a new runner it's more than likely you haven't asked yourself why you run. This question normally pops up when you're training for a race such as a 10K or another race that calls for a greater distance. It could crop up when your mind and body are in a state of flow, or what athletes like to call the *zone*. The question seems to come out of nowhere. It could be when your body is exhausted, and your mind is trying to trick you into stopping your run.

Running because you're a runner, in my opinion, is as good an answer as any. What tends to happen to runners after they accomplish a long-distance race is that they keep coming back for more races and pushing themselves further and further or try to beat their personal best records.

Your reason for running could be as simple as "I want to run a marathon because it's on my bucket list."

I had zero intention to run a marathon. In fact, most people who know me would have lost the bet if they said that one day I would run a marathon.

# Long Run Hacks

So why do we run? The deeper answer lies within each of us and normally doesn't surface until you've run for a while or you're pushing yourself to train for a long-distance race. I could answer the question better for myself after I had run my first half marathon.

The reason I run is that it makes me feel alive. I enjoy being exhausted after a long-distance run or race. Determining the reason you run can help reinvigorate you and get you through those long runs that sometimes you dread.

## Action steps:

- Find the reason you run to help reignite your passion for running.
- Answer the question: Do you run to train, to feel alive, to raise money for charity, to compete, to remain healthy, to lose weight, or another reason?

# Long Run Hacks

## Tip #3

### Find a Running Buddy

A running partner can help motivate you to get up and run on those days where you just don't want to make an effort. There are going to be days that you just don't jive with your body and your mind is sending out signals that it just doesn't want to run. Sometimes when your body doesn't want to run, even a running partner can't help you get up and run. But, if you have a partner they can hold you accountable in many ways.

First, scheduling your runs with a partner holds you more accountable not only to yourself and training but also to your running buddy. You tend to be much easier on yourself and your training goals than a running partner would be. Obviously, you need a motivating running partner, one that will help push you when you need that extra shove. Naturally, if you have a running partner and you renege on a scheduled run time, you will have to deal with the consequences of them being upset with you. If it's something that you've scheduled for yourself, you will find it easier to find excuses not to run for a given scheduled run.

Running partners can also help you by being a sounding board. You can ask them questions about running and their techniques. Partners sometimes can also help you troubleshoot causes of injury and injury prevention.

If your running buddy happens to be your spouse, then you are not only staying accountable to get your running in, but you are also getting to spend time with your spouse.

You don't have to run with someone to be your accountability running partner. For instance, if a couple has young kids it's next to impossible to find time for the couple to run together. The couple can make a schedule and swap running shifts so that each partner can get their complete run.

Several websites cater to accountability partnering for goals such as running, weight loss, alcohol abuse, etc. On these websites, you can view profiles and see who is looking for a remote accountability partner. You can customize how many times a week you want to "check-in" with your partner and what criteria and goals you want to set. At a bare minimum, in my opinion, partners should pick one day of the week and check in with each other weekly. The "check-in." can be an email system where one person sends an email and the other replies to satisfy the "check-in". Some partners would rather meet in person at a coffee shop for an hour or have a nice dinner and discuss each other's weekly progress. With the ease of video calling (i.e. Skype, FaceTime) partners can easily visually connect with one another no matter their location differences.

There are, several drawbacks to having a partner. One, if you or your partner don't take accountability seriously, this can not only break the partnership this could shatter a friendship. Secondly, if your partnership requires both of you to run together and one person slackens off, the accountability will fade away. Also, when choosing a physical running partner, you should have a few trial runs and ask your partner plenty of questions like pacing, 5k run times, half marathon run times, etc. so that each of you will know if it is a good fit. Being dishonest about your run times with your partner will quickly show up in the running efforts, so don't lie. Studies have found that even if one of the running partners is faster than the other, the slower runner helps the longer runner by making them slow down and get in volume on scheduled weekly long runs.

## <u>Action steps:</u>

- Have a few trial runs together with your physical running partners before committing to something more formal.
- Just "check-in" with someone and discuss each other's progress. You don't have to run with someone to physically have a partner.
- Remember running buddies can quickly get you out of a rut if you do not want to run. One drawback is when you are both stuck in a non-running rut you don't have anyone to help pull you out.

## Tip #4

### Ditch the Tech Gear

Every now and again, leave all your tech gadgets behind on a long run. I'm referring to things like your GPS watches, smart phones, ear buds, heart-rate monitors, drones, and any other tech props you may have amassed. Allow your body to absorb the ambient audio and visual scenery around you while you run. Concentrate on breathing techniques, form, and feet on the ground. Simply enjoy the run. This might be hard to accomplish if you are in the middle of a half marathon or marathon training plan and your pacing and tempo runs must be tracked in detail. If your training plan doesn't allow for this type of free, natural run, then move it to a rest day and go for a brisk walk or hike without the tech gear. Spending a day out in nature without the worry of your smart phone, music, or pace not only can give your body a break but it may also help to lower your stress levels. However, you should only walk, hike, or run, on a familiar trail or course so that you don't get lost. If you want to take it one step further you can test run some minimalistic shoes on your next natural run. If you're brave, you can go barefoot.

It's Sunday; you're sitting down to make out your running schedule for the week. Strategically you plan out your running days for the next seven days, stretching hours here and waking up early there. Monday comes, and it's your first run session of the week. You wake super early, before dawn, and realize your next scheduled race is months down the line. You don on your running gear for the appropriate weather, slip on your shoes and finally fasten down your tech ware. Stop! Put down the tech ware and take a step back. *Did this author just tell me to not wear my tech gear?* Hear me out. I'm not telling you to drop your tech gear during an important training schedule or on an important long run. I'm talking about not wearing your tracking ware for just one run - preferably during your off-season. *Absurd! Right?* Most runners, including myself, have a tough time taking a break from their tech.

In our current society, we live in an ever-growing digital world where we are into our devices all the time. In fact, *Glowface* is a new slang term to describe smart phone addicts. I believe we must give our minds and bodies a break from this constant volley of electronic waves and digital social interactions. I believe that social media possesses both good and evil qualities that if left unchecked could do more harm than good. What's the point? We all need to take a break from the computer, the TV, our phones, and of course our GPS tracking watches. Leave them by the door on your next run. If you must have a reference point before you run, check the clock as you head out and recheck the clock when you return. With this time, you can still roughly calculate your pace. However, remember: you need to run in a location where you already know the distance.

## **Action steps:**

- Leave your tech gear behind and go for a free natural run.
- If your schedule is too hectic, then go for a walk or hike to relax your mind.
- Don't ditch your tech gear during training. It's much easier to wait until your off-season to try this.

# Long Run Hacks

## Tip #5

### Share Your Running Moments via Social Media

With several different social network platforms available it's easy to start using each one as a vehicle for inspiration and motivation.

Posting runs or your running goals can help motivate you to stay on track through the times you don't feel like running. When you post a goal, it helps keep you accountable while at the same time allowing for positive feedback and motivation from your friends and society in general.

Platforms such as Instagram, if you have a lack of followers or if you already have a large follower's base, you can include hashtags in your post. For example, if you are currently training for a 10K, you can add *#10KTraining* as a hashtag, and it will show up in the hashtag groups that have articles with the same hashtag.

When you share via hashtags, anyone interested can view your post and either like or comment. They also may follow you, which will slowly help you build a follower base that can be used for motivation. Several apps, such as Nike Run Club, allow your friends on the platform, to cheer you on during an active run. Nike Run Club also allows for Facebook friends to be notified when you go for a run and, if they like your post, it sends you a live cheer if you carry your phone with you.

Social media sites could also help you on days you don't feel like putting on your running shoes. Simply add a post expressing your lack of motivation, and you can get motivated to get your butt in gear and head for the trails.

Facebook groups are also a wonderful place to find people interested in similar activities or lifestyles. There are hundreds of running groups. Some are private, and some are public. These groups include general running, women's running, charity running, half marathon running, running with dogs, etc. Some of the running groups act as a forum for help and motivation. Other groups take it one step further and participate in meet and greet runs.

MeetUp is another great social media site for people who have similar hobbies and interests. MeetUp allows you to search by interest and city and then join a group. Each interest group has a calendar that shows events and times, so you can attend the events to meet new people.

Long Run Hacks

## **Action steps:**

- Post achievements and goals to a social media website to help you maintain accountability and open the ability to be cheered on by your peers.
- Several apps can now be directly integrated with Facebook for in-app cheering.
- Use hashtags in your tweets when you post to Twitter and Instagram to build your following.

# Long Run Hacks

# Tip #6

## Music

Music is a great motivator to get you in the mood to start running and stay running. Music varies all over the board but, you are going to want to listen to something that is on the upbeat of the music spectrum. Rock and roll, heavy metal, pop, hip-hop, electronic, dance music or whatever style of music that gets your blood pumping is a fantastic way to jump-start your motivation. If you listen to the same playlist over and over, it might be time to add some new tracks. To get ideas, you can search Google for "Running Music 2018".

*Rock My Run* is a unique website and app that allows you to download premixed dance/high energy music associated with a specific tempo aligning with your heart rate, steps, or cadence. The app has 100s of workout stations and automatically determines what beat per minute tempo at which you are running. The only drawback with this type of app is that you must run with a smart phone.

Obviously, you can use your smart phone to simply look up running music on YouTube or Spotify and stream it for free. Amazon and Google Play also have music services that allow you to stream your music or download music you have purchased from these retailers. I don't run with my smart phone, so I download my music and playlists to my SAN Disk MP3 player that clips to my shorts or shirt. It's much lighter than a smart phone, and I don't have to hold or fasten my phone to

# Long Run Hacks

my arm. My GPS enabled Garmin Vivo Active keeps track of my pacing and running times.

Whatever source of music you use, you will probably perform significantly better with music in your ears.

# Long Run Hacks

## **Action steps:**

- Listen to upbeat music while you run.
- Focus better with music while running.
- Use Rock-My-Run as a great app to stream 100s of stations directly to your phone.

# Long Run Hacks

# Tip #7

## Recover Correctly - Trigger Balls and Foam Rollers

Taking care of your body after running long distances is essential. You can easily skip a long recovery period if you aren't running long distances.

When you start running longer distances during a running session, such as distances greater than five miles, you need to make sure that you have a good cool down and an even better recovery routine. Foam rollers, trigger balls, and canes help move around the facial tissue that sits on top of your muscles allowing the blood to flow better and more evenly around core muscle groups.

If you don't already own a foam roller, I highly suggest purchasing one. They come in many different shapes and sizes. The most common floor foam roller is one that you can easily lay your body on and "roll" back and forth. The diameter of foam rollers ranges from three inches to six inches. Some of the larger diameter foam rollers are primarily for your back, while the thinner foam rollers can be used to get to nook and crannies like between your shoulder blades.

The length of foam rollers varies based on the functionality of the foam roller. The 12-inch foam rollers are more compact and much easier to pack in a suitcase or throw in the back of your car. The 24-inch rollers are great for your extremities such as your legs and arms. The 36-inch foam rollers are best used for your back, your entire body, or to massage both of your legs at once.

The firmness of foam rollers also plays a big part in which one to buy. If you're a beginner, you might want to choose a roller that is less dense and has more play in the pressure that is applied to your body. Medium and firm types tend to be utilized by more experienced users for issues such as core stabilization or to put extra firm pressure on a set of muscles.

Some foam rollers also have dimples or trigger points on the outer surface. These dimples and triggers are designed to penetrate deeper layers of muscle and massage out extremely tight muscles groups on the body. Use caution using dimpled or trigger point foam rollers especially if you have never used them before. The deep massage and trigger point activation could be painful to inexperienced users.

A Trigger Ball is another form of muscle and facial massager. Just like the name implies, trigger balls can range in size from a golf ball all the way up to the size of a small cantaloupe.

Just as foam rollers have different shapes and sizes, so do Trigger Balls. Some of the trigger balls have dimples and/or various shapes on the ball that help dig deeper into sore and fatigued muscles to help stimulate facial movement and relieve muscle tensions.

The trigger ball is also ideal for taking with you when you travel due do its relatively small size and weight of the massager. A tennis ball acts as a decent trigger ball if you are on a budget. Avoid racquetballs because they are too squishy and baseballs because they are too large and hard.

# Long Run Hacks

## **<u>Action steps:</u>**

- Consider buying a foam roller to help work out kinks and tight muscles before and after running.
- Consider massage Canes and trigger balls. They can also be great tools to help relieve hard-to-get-to places on your body.
- Remember trigger balls and tennis balls are great to take on trips because you can just throw them in your suitcase.

## Tip #8

### Hire a Coach

Running Coaches can help you with different things such as speed work, dieting, weight loss, injury prevention and many other issues runners find themselves in. They can also help you with running long distances and dive into the reasons you are struggling with the long-distance run.

When you train for a half marathon, you must be able to complete several long runs during your training schedule to be able to run most of the race. What becomes difficult is when you're training for a marathon, and you must complete 18-22 mile runs during your running sessions toward the end of a marathon training schedule.

The reasons we struggle with long distance running varies widely. The reasons can range from depleted energy levels, motivation, physical cramping or pains, feeling under the weather, or simply just getting in the mood to start your long run.

When you select a coach make sure select the right coach for you. Regardless of what you're training goals are a good coach should ask you some important questions like the following:

1) What are your running goals?

2) How much time do you have to run on a daily, weekly, monthly schedule?

3) How much are you willing to spend?

4) What season is your favorite for training?

5) Do you have any history of running injuries or injuries in general?

6) What is your favorite type of workout?

7) What is your least favorite workout?

8) What is your proudest race? Why?

9) What are your running records?

10) What are your biggest challenges?

11) What kind of runner are you? (Do you run for fun/health benefits? Are you an intermediate runner, race competition runner, expert runner)?

12) On tough run days, what motivates you to push through them?

13) Why do you want to hire a coach?

14) What is the one thing on which you specifically need to work?

# Long Run Hacks

Most running coaches keep up with the latest news and trends in the community and sports science. If your goals aren't laid out, you could waste a lot of time and a lot of money. Make sure you know what you want the coach to help you accomplish.

## <u>Action steps:</u>

- Hire a running coach but make sure they are a good fit and can help you with your running goals?
- Make sure you settle on an hourly rate or maximum amount of money you are willing to spend. Running coaches can be expensive so.
- Check the RRCA.org list of certified coaches on their website based on your location.

## Tip #9

### Get Adequate Rest

You are better off missing a long run if your body hasn't had enough rest. Without adequate rest, your body is at a disadvantage before you even start running. You will have to seek out extra motivation to get your running gear on and your shoes on your feet.

Ask yourself this question. Do you run the day before a big race (excluding what I call an extremely light fidget run)? The answer is probably no. If you're running the day before a race, you need to reassess your running schedule because you are putting your physical body at a disadvantage.

You need to treat your long runs like a race-day run. This involves resting the night before a race or long run. Drink plenty of water, minimize alcohol consumption, and get plenty of rest.

The average adult needs about between seven and nine hours sleep a night. Catching a nap during the day can help on the nights that you aren't getting enough sleep.

Scientists have proven that you're able to catch up on some of your sleep. The more rest your body gets, the more motivated your body should be to finish your longer runs.

# Long Run Hacks

## Action steps:

- Get plenty of sleep, I advise between seven and nine hours.
- Rest the day before your long runs and rest for two days before a race.

# Tip #10

## Commit to Cross Training Once a Week

Cross-training is critical to help you endure your long run sessions. Many runners make the mistake of not cross training at all. When you cross-train, your body works muscles that aren't commonly used during your running sessions. Cross-training targets a muscle or muscle groups. Each set of muscles can then be conditioned with strength, endurance, balance, and flexibility or range of motion drills.

Strength training can help you sustain a longer run in numerous ways. First, when you lift weights that target your core such as your legs, back, and abdomen, you are strengthening the muscle that helps you maintain your posture in a good upright position when you run. If you've never experienced hunching over when you run, trust me it causes your gait cycle to get all out of whack and can cause premature cramping in the outer sides of the quadriceps muscle. When your upper body gets tired of holding an upright position due to a long exertion run, the other parts of your physical body must help support the muscles that have reached fatigue. When the secondary muscles kick in to help you stay afloat, they too then become quickly fatigued causing almost instant cramping in parts of your legs that you didn't think could cramp.

Endurance cross training can help lengthen the time it takes your muscles to fatigue. For instances, holding a lunge for a minute per leg can be a terrific way to give your muscles prolonged endurance. Also, you could hold a squat for a minute as well. Upper body endurance can be achieved by performing light-weight reps with an exercise. Some examples are chest press, medicine ball push-ups, seated rows, barbell curls, dumbbell curls. For your leg endurance training, you can perform lightweight multiple rep leg curls, leg extensions, lunges, and squats.

Balance cross training is simple to perform and can be done from virtually any location. Stand on one leg for two minutes and then stand on the other leg for another two minutes. Some of the yoga poses that require balance are the crane pose, firefly pose, and peacock pose just to name a few. Not only does yoga help with balance and strength it also helps with your breathing which is critical in mastering for any long duration sport. Mastering your breathing will help you with breathing economy during a long run.

To gain flexibility for your legs, stretching plays a key part in accomplishing this. Before you static stretch (stretching at rest), make sure your legs are slightly warmed up. Warm up by performing a light jog or by doing a few dynamic stretching drills such as knee raises or over-outs. A few of the most beneficial stretches for runners are the quad stretch, hamstring and calf stretch, and the hurdle stretch.

## Action steps:

- Try to incorporate at least one session of each of the following strength and endurance, flexibility, and balance.
- By cross-training, you are helping your body maintain a solid upright position during a long run and helping to strengthen non-running muscles that you don't use during your longer running sessions.

# Long Run Hacks

# Tip #11

## Change Your Running Time

Another way to help motivate you is to change up your routine by changing the time of day you run. Some runners prefer to run in the wee hours of the morning before the sun comes up. While others enjoy running later in the day. When the temperature is decent, and you don't have to worry about extreme bouts of hot and wintry weather, it's much easier to change up your time of the day that you train. If you do live in a place where temperatures are extreme, you can still change up your run times, but you might prefer to do it a gym.

Runners that are pressed for time might have to split their long runs in half. For instance, if a runner's training schedule calls for a mile run. They could run the first session on a lunch break and a second session in the evening when they get home.

If your training for a half marathon I recommend that you have at least three long-running sessions that last at least two hours or the appropriate running distance. You can split some of the long-distance runs up, but don't split them all up. Your body needs to physically and mentally feel the impact and effects of a long duration run that simulates what a half marathon race will feel like. That's why we train so that our bodies can grow accustomed to the feeling of long duration runs.

# Long Run Hacks

## Action steps:

- Run at night after the sun settles.
- Run indoors on a treadmill.
- Run in the morning before the sun rises above the horizon.
- Take a mid-afternoon run on your lunch break.
- If you're pressed for time, split up a long run.

## Tip #12

### Meditation

Meditation can also be utilized to help motivate you to run. During meditation, you are constantly attempting to suppress thoughts and concentrate on nothing except for the form of your breathing. When negative thoughts about running pop up in your mind consider taking an eight-minute meditation session to help relieve some of the negative and disbelieving thoughts about going on a run. Meditation can also help clear your thoughts before a race or an event.

Victor Davich, author of *8 Minute Meditation Expanded: Quiet Your Mind. Change Your Life,* explains that you don't require hours of time or rigid ancient postures to benefit from meditation. I read Davich's book and was able to implement simple meditation within an eight-minute session. Was it a life-changing experience and heightened enlightenment? No. It did, however, allow me to refocus my energies and suppress my mind's non-motivational sneak attacks. Is meditation hard at first? Sure, it takes practice, but even practicing meditation is useful in improving your focus skills. You can also use the meditation for other aspects of your life. For instances, you can meditate at work if your feeling stressed out. You can meditate at night to help you wind down for the day. Or you can meditate in the morning to help start off your day in a more positive and refreshed manner.

# Long Run Hacks

## Action steps:

- Try meditation before a long run to help clear your mind and motivate you.
- Focus on deep breathing when meditating.

## Tip #13

### Schedule Your Success

When we were kids and running around without a clue of what time it was or what we had to do next, we somehow were forced to transition into the adult world and had more responsibilities thrown at us.

If you feel like I do, you can remember that when you were a kid, outside school. You can recall when you wanted to do something, like build a fort, you built it. You didn't think about when you had to make dinner, or when you had to pick up the kids; you just let your imagination flow and zone out at the moment.

As adults, we all look for that moment where we just turn off outside distraction and zone in and focus with razor-sharp precision on the task at hand.

Adults have a much more tough time finding those, flow or zone states partially because we are so busy. In fact, on our daily routine if you wrote down everything you did for one solid week every hour you would be surprised at how much time was wasted just thinking about what you need to get done.

As kids, we didn't have to worry about this kind of stuff. At some point as a productive adult, we started to have to use a calendar or, at the bare minimum, make some list to keep your mind and energy focused in the right direction.

# Long Run Hacks

To run a 10K, half marathon, or marathon, you must schedule your running into your adult life. Scheduling your runs, if you're serious about running, needs to be a priority somewhere in your weekly schedule.

I'm not talking about running every day. In fact, running every day is a sure way to bring on unnecessary injuries quickly. Endless counts of research show us that if you are participating in long distance running, running more than four days a week starts to have a law of diminishing returns effect.

In other words, for each additional day and mile you jog beyond four days, your body is getting less and less benefit. At a minimum, you should be resting at least one day from running. I'm not saying not to exercise at all. I'm saying that you should take a break from running in the form of some other type of exercise such as walking, cycling, ply metrics (jumping), yoga, kettle bell workouts, etc.

When you write down your schedule on a planner or app, you are creating a habit of scheduling your runs, which is a fantastic way to jump-start the habit before acting on the habit. Try to remember to write down your running schedule daily if needed to help it stick as an important habit.

Scheduling your daily activities other than just running at least the night before helps to ensure that you are laser focused on what you wish to accomplish the next day.

# Long Run Hacks

Some people's list might be so long it would make our head spin. I would focus on a bare minimum of at least three goals that you wish to accomplish the next day. I wouldn't push past five big goals. I normally choose one activity for exercise, one to three for work productivity, and one for personal relationships.

Depending on how far along you are in your running career, determines how disciplined your running habits are. I've been running for close to two years now and, I no longer need to use running as one of my top three goals to accomplish the next day.

One last thing on running, if you're not getting paid to run for a living (as a professional), then you're running shouldn't completely dictate your life.

Try to stick to a running schedule as much as humanly possible, however, don't forget that if your partner or spouse isn't a runner, then sometimes it's hard for them to understand a runner's training schedule - truly. All I'm saying is don't let your running schedule cripple other parts of your life.

# Long Run Hacks

## Action steps:

- Take time out of each day to start scheduling your runs.
- Try to do it before your work week starting to get you through Monday grinds. Some people find it easier to schedule on a weekly basis like on a Saturday or Sunday.
- Physically schedule your runs by writing them down as much as possible, this makes it more likely you will make it a habit.
- Don't let your training schedule take a stranglehold on your life.

## Tip #14

### Try to Beat a Personal Best

Trying to beat a personal best is one of the best ways to motivate you to run. It doesn't matter what race distance you are trying to beat whether it's a one mile, 5k, 10k, 15k, half marathon, or full marathon, attempting to beat your personal best is great to revive dull running sessions.

Write down your personal best for the distance you want to crush. Secondly, write down what time you want to be your new personal best. In almost every instance of trying to beat a personal best running time, you need to perform some speed work.

To have enough time to try to beat a personal best, you need to set aside a certain number of weeks to train so that your body can begin to get used to training at its new threshold. By allowing your body to train at its new threshold, you normally begin to feel less fatigued as you continue to run at your new raised level of effort.

If after several weeks of training, you don't see an increase in your threshold then you could be doing some things wrong. Six reasons why you might not be increasing your speed are your weight, injuries, intervals not being tough enough, poor diet, underlying medical conditions, and lack of rest.

First, to increase your speed, you need to make sure that you are on the losing side of weight or at a bare minimum, the maintaining side. If you're an advent runner you probably run at least a few times a week. Since you exercise quite often your body needs fuel to help rebuild your muscles and your glycogen store. Just because you run doesn't mean that you go to all-you-can-eat buffets after running sessions (in my opinion, you should never eat at a buffet).

Running your intervals hard enough might be another reason why your speed isn't increasing. Depending on how much of a distance run you are trying to increase your speed with your interval session should dynamically change. For instance, if you're trying to increase your 5K running speed then your interval distance should be around 200 meters (1/8 mile). With 200 meters you can run a 1/8 at an increased pace and then walk or jog 1/8 mile then repeat the process. Each 1/8 interval run should become more and more taxing on your body. Each week you add on another interval cycle. For instance, if you are starting out running a four-interval cycle then the following week you should increase your interval cycle to 5 total. Progressing each week by one cycle until you are up at around 8-10 total interval cycles. Also, you only need to add one of these interval training sessions per week. Anymore and you could flat line or negate your training sessions by overtraining.

Obviously, in situations where medical conditions are out of your control it is not recommended for you to ignore advice from a doctor not to undergo rigorous exercising. If you feel that your doctor might be giving you ill advice, then go get a second opinion or even a third opinion. If you do seek additional opinions from licensed physicians, don't tell them that this is a second opinion appointment. To receive an unbiased opinion, you need to keep everything hush-hush, just pretend it's the first time you have seen someone about your specific condition.

The same goes for injuries as for medical conditions. If you're hurt, you're better off letting the injury heal than to force yourself to drudge through workouts in pain. When I mean pain, I'm talking about pain that hurts so bad that you must stop your activity because to exercise further would make it unbearable to withstand more pain.

I'm not talking about your calf muscles getting cramps or your legs tightening up. Both issues can be resolved by stretching during the middle of a run. I'm referring to sharp, debilitating pains that pierce your muscles and almost bring you to tears.

Some people's thresholds of pain are higher than others. We all should know our bodies well enough to be able to call it quits if you hear a snap or pop in your knee and you fall to the ground instantly. That could be a possible dislocation or worse an MCL or ACL tear.

Also, as we age, our bodies become even more susceptible to injury so listening to your body is way more important than trying to trudge through your pains. If you don't believe me, ask someone who has had a knee replacement surgery or an ACL/MCL tear.

The procedure to fix both is fairly streamlined nowadays. However, the surgery is the easy part. The real pain kicks in when you must go through the rehabilitation process.

I know first-hand about ACL tears. My brother, a soccer goalkeeper, tore his ACL in both knees. His surgery went fine. Part of his rehabilitation process involved his leg being hooked up to a machine that lifts and lowers his leg for several hours a day bending at the knee to help strengthen his leg. The heavy pain medication did nothing to alleviate his pain during his rehabilitation process.

Finally, not getting enough sleep can wreak havoc on every part of your life including your important exercise routines. You hear repeatedly about how the average adult human needs between seven and eight hours of sleep or more - right? Well, the data is true for the most part.

Lately, there have been small trends and scientists telling us that we would be better off letting our bodies wake themselves up rather than using an alarm clock. Their argument is that when you force yourself to wake up, you could be interrupting your most important sleep cycle, which is the second round of deep sleep.

For instance, let's pretend that Adult #1 only gets seven hours sleep and his alarm wakes up right after his body has completed the second round of deep sleep. Adult #2 gets 8.5 hours of sleep but for some reason, his body is catching up on a lack of sleep, and when his alarm wakes him up he is still in his second-deep sleep cycle.

Which adult will feel more rested? Adult #1 even though he didn't get as much sleep as Adult #2. Adult #1 can pop up out of bed and hit the ground running whereas Adult #2 is probably still groggy.

We have all experienced it before, it's Saturday, and we wake up tired then go back to bed for an hour or so. What is really happening is our body still needs time to finish its sleep cycle, so you snooze for a while longer then wake up feeling more rested. Make sure that you are getting the right amount of rest to help repair your muscles especially if you're a long-distance runner.

## Action steps:

- Aim for better and faster goals. It is an effortless way to help boost running motivation
- If you struggle with beating a personal best record, investigate one of these factors: weight, injuries, intervals not being tough enough, underlying medical conditions, and lack of rest.

## Tip #15

### Log Your Runs

Just like scheduling your runs helps form a habit of writing down your goals and sticking to them, keeping a running log will help you punch through the days of not wanting to hit the pavement or trail.

Running logs successfully reflect the scheduling of your runs. When you have a run scheduled and you accomplish it make sure you check it off your list and add any notes to it such as severe weather, too cold, ran like the wind, etc. When you get serious about running, you will probably want to add more fields and information to the log.

Several running apps allow you to use almost countless numbers of fields. However, remember that the simpler you keep your log the more likely you will use it to your benefit.

Some people need the ability to log as much information as possible while others only need the bare minimum of fields to get a good grasp of their running history. At a bare minimum I recommend logging the:

Date:
Time:
Training Week: (e.g. Week #1 of 6 for a 5k):
Location:
Pace (min/Mile):
Total Run Time:

Other fields you might want to consider include:

Cadence (Strides Per Minute):
Weather:
Average Pace:
Static Stretching (warm-up):
Static Stretching Type:
Post Stretching:
Post Stretching type:
How your body feels before running:
How your body feels after running:

Running logs not only show you how you performed over a certain time frame, but they can also show you how far you have come in your running career. Logs also help create a sense of accomplishment and help push you in the direction of getting you out the door and on to your long runs.

By logging your runs, you are helping to form the habit of recording your performance during a run. Who cares if it's a lousy run. Record it anyway. There is no way to improve your running capability unless you know how you're performing. Also, if you keep an adequate running log, you can take the log to your running coach so that he or she can see your past running history. A running coach will be able to look at your log and see what types of running should be added or changed.

Finally, another reason to log your runs is to help avoid what experts call "black hole" training. Black hole training is going out and doing the same exact run every single day four days a week.

Your body gets used to doing that run, and you slowly start getting less and less benefit from the same workout. You are still burning calories, but if you change up your running routine a little bit, by looking at your activity log, you can throw diverse types of runs in such as sprinting for 10 seconds at the end of one of your runs.

By making simple changes such as these, you can help quell any flailing motivation to run. Your body will also benefit from changes in your routine because your body will be using different muscle groups.

## <u>Action steps:</u>

- Keep a log of your runs. It doesn't have to be detailed at first just simple things such as distance, time, and pace.
- Review your running log at least once a week to see where you might need to tweak your routines.
- Give your log to a coach so that he or she can see where to make improvements.

## Tip #16

### Remember Why You Started Running

Do you remember the first time you started running? Your reasons could have been as simple as wanting to:

- Get in better physical shape
- Run a 5K race
- Run a 10K race
- Run a half marathon or marathon
- Give to a worthy cause
- Prove to yourself that you can be a runner
- Become faster
- Win a medal
- Change up your exercise routine
- Run for the sake of running

The list goes on and on as to why you may have started to run. Whatever the reason, you decided to start running visualize it. Close your eyes and live in that visualization for a few minutes. See yourself immersed in the middle of your vision.

If your vision has changed since you first started running that's fine. The reasons you start doing things often change into other reasons and goals. If you've progressed in your running without injury, you'll naturally take on bigger goals and bigger races. For example, I started running so that I could complete a half marathon. When I set out to complete my first half marathon, I had no intentions on even considering running a full marathon. After I completed my first half marathon, I realized that I just ran half way to a marathon.

I thought, I've already trained my body to run 13.1 miles. I can adjust my schedule and train another eight weeks so that I can be ready for a full marathon - and that's what I did. Sometimes it's hard to see where the path takes you because of where you're at on the actual path. If I hadn't trained for a half marathon, I wouldn't have seen the path to running a full marathon.

Long Run Hacks

## **Action steps:**

- Ask yourself why you started running
- Determine the reason you run and use that to help motivate you on your long runs.

# Long Run Hacks

# Tip #17

## Visualize Success - Victory Board

When the going gets tough, the tough get running. Visualizing your success is a key component in helping your mind realize that you can accomplish this task. The pounding of the pavement is just one of the aspects of running. Your mind plays an almost equal part in determining your long term running success. Training your mind just as you are training your body helps improve the odds that you will finish a run or race successfully.

Two ways to help visualize your running triumphs could be visualizing affirmations to improve and creating a vision board or wall. An affirmation is a daily repeat such as "I will complete my half marathon training." By taking this one step further and visualizing it, you are helping to merge the audio with the visual part of showing your mind success.

To successfully visualize your affirmations, close your eyes and repeat the affirmation out loud while creating an image in your head. Visual affirmations are best used right before a race or a long run. Also, another exciting time to repeat this routine is in the morning before you do anything else and the last action you perform before going to bed. Studies have shown that when you sleep your mind tends to think and dream about the last thing you were thinking about before going to bed.

# Long Run Hacks

Before you hit the pavement for your long run, stop and take a few minutes to visualize your long run success. This exercise takes about five minutes and you can even couple this with your warm-up routine. First, close your eyes for two minutes and just concentrate on your breathing. Try to push everything out of your mind. After two minutes begin to visualize you on your long run. Next, visualize finishing the long run and how good it felt to be done with the race. Don't forget while performing this visualization to practice steady deep inhales and exhales. Your steady deep breathing during visualization should be the same breathing utilized during your longer runs.

The alternative is a Vision Board. It is just as it sounds. Visions, dreams, and goals can be placed on a board for you to refer to often throughout the day. Create a board or wall of visions that depicts your future success.

Your vision board doesn't have to contain only running successes. You can place any vision that you want to come true on the board, like a picture of your high school self for weight loss motivation. A picture of a dream car or dream house can also be placed on the board. You might consider making two of them. One vision board can be placed in your house or car. Another vision board can be placed where you work.

The smaller you make the vision board, the better off you will be. A smaller vision board will help you narrow what your mind sees daily. Your visions should be specific, such as you crossing a marathon finish line.

# Long Run Hacks

Physically cut out a picture of yourself and a picture of the finish line and place them on your board. Try to limit your vision board to no more than four or five items so that your mind isn't too scattered when you look at your board. For instance, a house, a car, a career vision, a personal vision, and maybe a family vision would be perfect for a vision board. Ultimately, it's up to you to decide what goes on there.

I tend to try to stuff my visions onto an index card. Yes, I know it's small, however, it makes you do some creative thinking and shrinking to put the stuff on the index card. Index cards work great for me because they are super easy to travel with. Take the time to look at your vision at least once in the morning and once in the evening. Stick with the habit for at least two weeks and assess if the vision board has helped you at all.

## **Action steps:**

- Consider making a vision board to help motivate yourself.
- Limit your vision board to no more than five items or visions.
- Refer to your vision board in the morning and the evening at a minimum.

## Tip #18

### Trick Your Mind

Sometimes the mind is the only thing between you and getting you charged to complete your long run. Like I've said before, your mind is half the battle when it comes to completing and pushing through long distance endurance running.

When thoughts creep into your mind such as, "I can't run any further" and "I'm too tired to finish the run," it's your mind telling you to slow down. Sometimes when your mind acts this way, it's due to a lack of energy.

When your body is physically tired, your legs will lock up in the form of muscle cramps. If you're continually experiencing mental fatigue when you're running, you might need to start logging how many calories you are eating before you run. If your runs last beyond 90 minutes, then make sure that you are refuelling often and getting a minimum of 250 calories an hour to sustain your energy levels. Why 250 calories? Your body, on average, can only assimilate approximately 250 calories an hour. If you attempt to consume more than your body can assimilate, then you're putting in excess food that might make you sick.

If you want to try and trick your mind into running further start with a few of these simple tricks:

- Look at how many more miles are left instead of how many miles you've run.

# Long Run Hacks

- Tell your mind that you will run one more mile and then you will walk for one minute.
- If you're trying to motivate yourself to start running, try telling yourself that you will run for five minutes or half a mile. Most of the time you will squash your mind's lack of motivation and keep running.
- Repeat affirmations such as, "I'm a runner, "I will finish my runs for the day."
- Visualize yourself not being tired.
- Pretend that you have a magic hook and then place it on a runner in front of you. The runner will tow you along. (Yeah, this one is a last resort, but you would be surprised how easily you can trick your mind for short periods of time).

Long Run Hacks

## **Action steps:**

- Make sure that you are running with enough fuel in your body. Mental fatigue is often a sign of a lack of energy,
- Try simple mind tricks such as telling yourself that you are just going to run for five minutes.
- Repeat your affirmations when your energy and mind feel fatigued.

# Long Run Hacks

## Tip #19

### <u>Reward yourself</u>

Setup a simple reward system that allows you some occasional indulgence. You can design a rewards system that works on a daily or weekly basis.

I find it makes more sense just to reward the longer runs since, the shorter runs should be easier to push through. I would discourage linking your rewards to food, although for some people this might be the best way to keep you motivated to complete your long run for the week.

I give myself slack when it comes to food. If I exercise at least four times a week, which may or may not include running, I allow myself at least one day where I can slack on my meals and not worry about the calories.

The one food group that I try to minimize every day is carbohydrate like bread and chips. I will eat sushi rolls, which include lots of rice (yikes - extra carbs), but this is on my "let loose" day or cheat day where I get to take off the dietary shackles as a reward for my exercising efforts.

Other rewards can be tied directly to your long run, such as completing a 10-mile long run might constitute allowing yourself to see a movie on the weekend. Maybe you reward yourself monthly when you complete all your long runs for the month. The possibilities are unlimited. You could also allow yourself to get a massage if you complete your exercise goals for a given week.

One thing that I don't recommend is tying your running to a harmful reward, such as smoking a cigarette or drinking a 12-pack of beer. This should be extremely obvious, and I'm not here to lecture you. I'm just pointing out that you might want the reward to be more positive such as completing four straight weeks of running could result in a treat for yourself.

If a positive reward system doesn't work, you can set up a negative reinforcement system. If you don't make a run, you could donate a certain amount of money to a charity. Both positive and negative motivation system can work but you obviously must be honest with yourself, or they will fail.

## **Action steps:**

- Setup a simple rewards system.
- Write down on your running log the reward if you run for four days for one week.
- Make the rewards as frequent as daily but don't try to reward yourself multiple times in one day. Over-rewarding yourself can lead to diminishing returns on the reward itself. This could make the reward lose its strength in motivating you to act.

# Long Run Hacks

## Tip #20

### Fartlek

Fartlek, created by Gösta Holmér, means "speed play." It's like interval training except the intervals can be variable instead of consistent. An example of a running Fartlek would be run to the nearest tree then recover, turn left, now sprint to the nearest playground equipment, now walk for one minute to recover, jog backwards to the park bench, recover for one minute, etc. The essence of Fartlek helps both the mind and the physical body in many ways. Fartlek will help up break up your daily routines, engage both aerobic and anaerobic cardiovascular exercise, and add a game-like training session to your exercise routine. On a day that you are having trouble motivating yourself to run you might just randomly do Fartleks instead of your run. One word of caution, a Fartlek run shouldn't be substituted for a long-distance run.

First, Fartlek will help you break up your day to day routines of the same run or the same cycling. This will not only aid your mental state by refreshing a run or bike session with new sceneries and new tasks for your mind to tackle, but it will work new muscles in your body that you normally don't work during your day-to-day routine runs.

Secondly, by varying your physical drills, you can also change up the same old run routine. These physical drills could include jogging backwards, sideways running (almost like skipping), sideways cross-overs, jumping on a park bench then jumping off, which all change up your aerobic and anaerobic cardiovascular exercising.

Another wonderful way to use Fartleks is by creating a game-like training session with one of your running buddies or partners. You can also include an entire running club in the game-like session. Each runner alternates and calls out the new Fartlek goal and rest period and all participating runners engage in the Fartlek and try to beat the other runner. When playing the game, you obviously need to call out both the run and rest Fartlek goal. During the rest part of the Fartlek, another runner then picks a random Fartlek goal with a rest period. You keep rotating through so that each runner can pick at least one Fartlek goal and rest period. You would continue this until a certain pre-defined timed or distance goal is accomplished.

# Long Run Hacks

## **<u>Action steps:</u>**

- Start using Fartlek running techniques.
- If you have a buddy, try a couple of challenges or if you run in a club do a club challenge Fartlek.
- Try varying your Fartlek sessions between distance and timed goals.

# Long Run Hacks

## Bonus Tip #21

### Run with Someone Slower

Although the idea of running with someone slower during your long runs sounds counter intuitive, you would be surprised at how many benefits it offers both runners. First, your long runs are supposed to be about completing the long miles at a slower than normal marathon or half marathon pace. The slower runner will help lasso you back down to a slower running pace. Another great benefit of running with someone slow is that you get to be socially involved. When you are running your easy long run distance, you should be able to hold a conversation with a fellow runner. Also, you should be able to only breathe out of your nose during your runs. Another great benefit of running with someone slower is that it puts less stress mentally and physically on the body. Your legs already get a tough workout during the week during your base run sessions. Why not change it up a little bit and slow down the runs? Finally, you're helping another fellow runner by running with them. This serves as a great source of motivation to push you both of you through the tough long runs.

# Long Run Hacks

## **Action steps:**

- When you run with someone slower, you're helping yourself more than the fellow runner.
- Running with someone slower puts less stress on your legs.
- Your breathing economy should also increase when you are running at a slower pace.

**Bonus Tip #22**

## Check Your Running Form

When you run shorter distances such as a 5K, your bio-mechanical running form is not going to create any type of "form drag" on your performance. Also, I'm not advocating that you go out and purposefully try to change your striking technique or your overall form. However, your running form could be causing you to deplete more energy or let your body become more susceptible to running injury thus causing you and your long runs to suffer. By analyzing the foot strike, proper form, and extra luggage such as water bottles and phones, you might be able to help your legs stay safe and conserve a little bit more energy for your longer runs.

**Foot Strike**

First, study after study after study has been done and there is no evidence to support that one type of foot strike causes more injury than the other. The causes of injury are due to where the feet land in perspective to the body. If you are a sprinter then you will be using forefoot striking.

Three types of foot strikes:

Forefoot - the forefoot and toes land first on each step.

Midfoot - the midsole lands first.

Heel - the heel of the foot lands first. This is where the majority of runners fall into place. About 75% - 85% of all runners are heel strikers. This statistic depends on what source you reference or who you talk to. I myself am a heel striker.

What you want to avoid is continuous overstriding during a long run. The forefoot strikers are prone to overstriding. Olympic sprinters land on the forefoot and their foot lands out in front with each stride. To avoid overstriding your foot should land slightly in front and below your hip.

**Running Form**

First, no running form is perfect, however, there are some basic guidelines you should follow. Again, I'm not trying to get you to change your form. I'm simply trying to make you aware of ways that your energy might be draining out of you quicker than it should.

- Your Arms should be close to the side with a nice easy swing on each stride. Your arms don't need to extend beyond a 90-degree hinge.
- Spine straight.
- Body leaned slightly forward.
- Shoulders relaxed and slightly pushed back.
- Your nose should be the most forward appendage on your body.

Some possible running forms that might be draining your body or causing possible long-term injury, especially during longer runs where the miles and iterations of your form amplify:

- Running tense - This could be your shoulders or more commonly your arms. Some runners run with their arms tucked in and tightly toward their chest. By not allowing the arms to swing more freely your body is having to exert more energy for your muscles to hold your arms in place. An Example of this is what I call the football blocker where the arms are tucked in and parallel with the chest and it looks like they are blocking with every stride. If you run like this, again, I'm not telling you to change, just be aware that contracting the muscles like that requires more energy than an easy normal forward swing of the arm.

- Bouncing while you run - Unless you're running a specific drill such as knee hikes or runner hikes, you should avoid bouncing. Some runners don't know that they bounce. If you have a feeling that you might bounce when you run, you need to have someone videotape you for a minute or two running. When you bounce mile after mile on long runs, your body is springing up at a higher distance from the ground and coming down with more force on impact. This repetition repeatedly causes more energy exertion and the possibility of injury.

## Extra Baggage

Your extra baggage could be causing an imbalance with your running gait cycle. If you run with a phone especially over long distances (5+ miles) try to wear the armband on the upper part of your bicep and not down along the forearm. Even though a phone doesn't weight that much, mile after mile can add up and one side of your body might be slightly overcompensating for the difference in weight.

Also, make sure you're switching your phone placement between different arms every other run.

If you hold your phone in your hand, make sure to switch hands every mile or every 5 minutes or so. The same goes for a handheld running water bottle.

Hydration belts worn at the waste might be the best place to store your extra baggage. Some belts even have room for your phone to sit on your upper tail bone. A hydration belt is a good solution because it is worn on a part of the body that doesn't have much movement while you're running. If you do wear a belt, make sure you try to evenly distribute the weight across the belt.

A hydration pack is probably one of the best ways to carry your water and even phone. It sits on your back and it's securely fastened to your body with minimal movement. The weight is evenly distributed across the back and you don't have any imbalance.

## <u>Action steps:</u>

- Become aware of your running form.
- If you do start noticing a flaw in your form, take micro steps to fix the issue.
- Do not try to apply an immediate fix if you want to change the way your foot strikes the ground. If you want to slowly change your foot strike, I recommend talking to a running coach. Remember, there is no debilitating physical difference between what type of foot striker you are unless you overstride over long distances.

# Long Run Hacks

## Bonus Tip #23

### Split Up Your Long Runs

Recent scientific evidence has concluded that you receive no additional aerobic or physical gains from running more than three hours in one training session. Many marathoners fall into the category of needing to run at least three different sessions of 18 to 22 miles during a marathon training cycle. Unless you are an elite or above average runner you more than likely will not be able to run 22 miles within three hours. What do you if you fall into this category? You split up the run.

First of all you need to determine how many miles you can easily run within three hours. Let's say for example that you can only run 5 miles an hour which is a total of 15 miles after three hours and you need to run 18 hours. What you can do is run 40% of the miles required, which would be 7 miles (rounded) the day before your long run. Do not take your typical day off between these two runs. On the next consecutive day run the remainder of the miles which in this case would be 11 miles on your long run session. Although you aren't modeling an identical marathon run, your mind and body will be fatigued which is modeling what happens around mile twenty of a marathon. Apply this method to your half marathon or marathon training cycle no matter how slow you run. Remember that half marathon, and marathon training is a mind game as much as it is a physical battle to get to the finish line!

## <u>Action steps:</u>

- Split up your long runs by running 40% of your long run requirement the day before your long run.
- Run the remaining 60% of your long run the next consecutive day.
- If you split up your long runs, do not take a day off between your long run split.

## Conclusion

As runners, we all suffer from a lack of motivation from time to time. All runners at one point or another will experience a bad or lousy run. The enormous difference between a veteran runner and a new runner is the veteran knows that lousy runs happen from time to time. While new runners, might simply give up and never return to running. If you're new to running, I don't want this to happen to you. If you can't find yourself with enough motivation to complete a long run, shake off the run as simply a lousy run. Forgive yourself and don't look back. The key differences between experienced runners and new runners is that they simply didn't give up the first time they had a lousy run. To all runners I'm wishing you many long run successes in your future.

# Long Run Hacks

## Please Review My Book

Thanks for reading! If you've enjoyed this book, please let me know how I can make this book better. Other shoppers on Amazon rely on ratings so that it can save them valuable time when shopping for new eBooks. I take the time to read every review so that I can change and update this book based on reviewer feedback.

Click here to review book

If you've just finished a race and you want someone to tell, send me an email. I would be delighted to hear from you.

**Follow me on Facebook and Twitter:**

Twitter: @BeginR2FinishR

Facebook: facebook.com/BeginnerToFinisher/

Website: www.halfmarathonforbeginners.com

Email: scottmorton@halfmarathonforbeginners.com

## What's next?

If you've followed me through the Beginner to Finisher Series, this concludes book #5. Consider this book a prerequisite to training for a marathon. Since the long runs will be the most time consuming and enduring elements of a marathon training schedule, it's worth having every tool in the toolbox to get you past the tough runs.

The next book in the series will be an extensive walkthrough of my first and second marathons while including training schedules to get you to the marathon finish line in 18 weeks. This is where most people call it quits before they journey onto marathon training. From my experience, I still to this date, have never felt anything like the achievement of crossing the marathon finish line. For weeks after the race and possibly for the rest of your life you will see things in a much different perspective. Goals, obstacles, road blocks can all be achieved, pushed passed, and walked around. I do hope one day you will find yourself standing at the marathon finish line flooded with emotional victory. Until then run long, hard, and safe.

## Sign Up for Tips, Blogs, and eBook Releases

To receive running tips, blogs, and eBook releases go to http://B2F.GR8.com and sign up with your name and email address.

# Long Run Hacks

For a special sneak peek of,
*5K Fury: 10 Proven Steps to Get You to the Finish Line in 9 weeks or less!*
(Book #2 in the Series Beginner to Finisher),
turn to the next page.

Touch here to purchase.

## Motivation

Why do some people finish marathons and other don't? I believe it comes down to self-motivation and determination. Self-motivation, while probably the strongest of any other form of motivation, is not the only source of motivation. There are several different types of motivation. Three types of motivation that I believe are the most influential come from social media, running partners and yourself.

## Social Media

Social media can help keep you focused and motivated by your circle of friends. You can post running times and screenshots of your runs to social media to let your circle of friends comment and cheer you on. Social media will help perk you up when you have a day that you just don't feel like running.

## Running Partners

Running partners are the next best thing to yourself keeping you motivated. They train with you. They give you feedback. They help you stay on pace. They push you when you have no more energy. Partners also help you stay accountable for following through with your goal. One caveat to a running partner is that if they lack self-motivation, they aren't going to be of much help motivating you.

## Yourself

Self-motivation is by far the most powerful source of motivation. You know yourself better than anyone else. You are custom to knowing how your mind and body work. If you don't feel like running one day, tell yourself that you will just run a half a mile. After you run a half mile, tell yourself that you will just run one mile. By pushing yourself just a little bit, you can trick your mind into running.

Your motivation could be to get healthy and fit. Also, you could be motivated just to prove to yourself that you can finish a 5K or to donate to a worthy cause. Whatever the motivation is, you and only you will finish the race.

Touch here to purchase.
*5K Fury: 10 Proven Steps to Get You to the Finish Line in 9 weeks or less!*

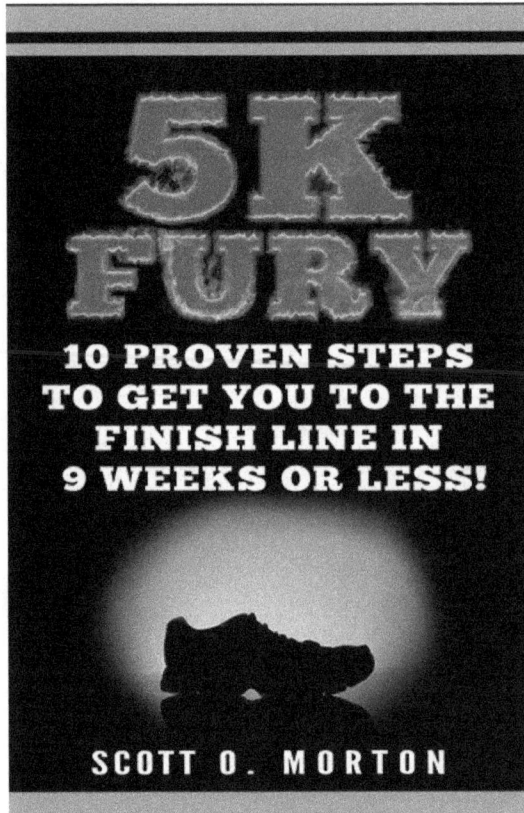

For a special sneak peek of,
*10K Titan: Push Beyond the 5K in 6 Weeks or Less!,*
(Book #3 in the Series Beginner to Finisher),
turn to the next page.


Touch here to purchase eBook version

## Fear of Running Far

New runners fear running past the distance of a 5K (3.1 miles). Why do we fear running longer distances? Here is a list of some of the reasons we might tell ourselves as to why we don't attempt to run past 3.1 miles:

- I'm not a runner.
- I'm not a long-distance runner.
- I fear that my body might not make it.
- I fear I might get injured.
- There is no way I can run that far and for that long.
- I can't run that far.
- I'm too overweight.
- I'm too out of shape.
- I'm too old.

The list goes well beyond some of the reasons listed above as to why we might be holding ourselves back from running the distance of a 10K. There are too many "I can't"s above. You have to shake loose the phrase, "I can't." That phrase poisons your mind with disbelief even before you get started.

Touch here to purchase eBook version

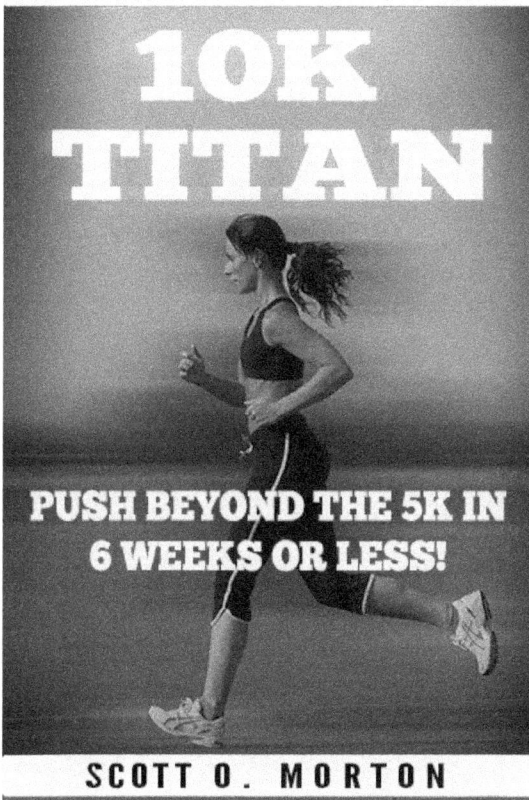

# Long Run Hacks

For a special sneak peek of,
*Beginner's Guide to Half Marathons: A Simple Step-By-Step Solution to Get You to the Finish Line in 12 Weeks!*
(Book #4 in the Series Beginner to Finisher),
turn to the next page.

## *Beginner's Guide to Half Marathons* has become an Amazon #1 Bestseller.

Touch here to purchase eBook version

Touch here to purchase the paperback version

Touch here to purchase the audiobook version

# Long Run Hacks

The runner's mindset. Getting past the fear of running 13.1 miles is one of the biggest hurdles of completing a half marathon. I'm going to let you in on a big secret that helped me get past my fear of having to run 13.1 miles. The secret is that most runners don't run the entire 13.1 miles. Wow, what a secret. It's true. The super athletes and other runners trying to beat their personal best records might very well run the entire race. However, I have completed three half marathons and one full marathon, and most runners will walk through the water/aid stations along the course. Once I realized that you don't have to run the entire distance, the fear of running a half marathon vanished, instantly. My mind had found a chink in the armor. Once I exploited the weakness of the 13.1 half marathon beast, my mindset changed forever on long distance running. This same technique allowed me to complete a marathon as well. Someone reading this right now is probably saying, "He's probably been running for a long time." I was able to complete three half marathons and one full marathon over the course of a year. I began in May 2016 and completed my third half marathon on April 22, 2017, at the age of 43 with no prior long distance running experience whatsoever. I'm by no means a super athlete, just an average person with high beliefs that I could finish a half marathon. I hope that this encourages you to finish your first half marathon no matter what age you begin at. If I can do it, so can you.

Finishing a 5K or a 10K can be easily accomplished with little or no training at all. If your goal is to run or walk/run a half marathon, then you must tell yourself that you are a runner. You are no longer running for the sake of exercise. You are running to train your body to complete your first half marathon. You are now training for a half marathon.

Many things that I go over in this book are solely my opinion. Every training schedule discussed within this book has been used by me to complete three half marathons and a full marathon. There are several different schools of thought when it comes to how much running per week it takes to train for a half marathon. There are different nutrition guides, shoe strategies, running miles per week, etc. There is, however, one common thing agreed upon by almost all runners - you must believe in yourself and believe that you are a runner. Without this firmly ingrained in your head, you won't make it past mile nine, and you won't make it to the finish line. I'm not telling you this to discourage you. I'm telling you this to prepare you for the mental battle of running. One week at a time, one day at a time, one mile at a time, and one step at a time will get you to the half marathon finish line.

Touch here to purchase eBook version

Touch here to purchase the paperback version

Touch here to purchase the audiobook version

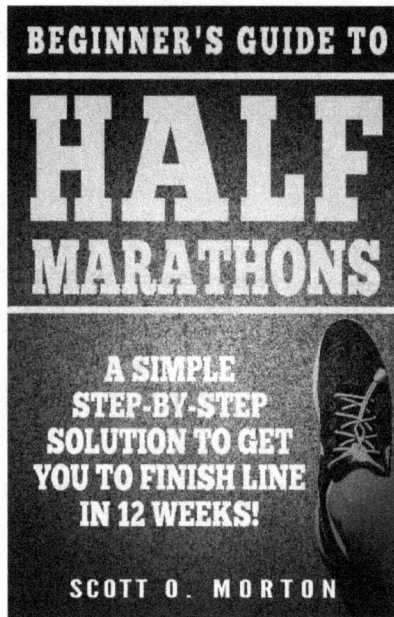

## Other Books by Scott Oscar Morton

If you would like to know when I publish my new eBook releases, please **sign up by clicking here**. You can read all these eBooks for **FREE with Kindle Unlimited**. **Click on the book titles below to buy or read with Kindle Unlimited.**

### Beginner to Finisher Series:

### Available Now:

**Book 1:** *Why New Runners Fail: 26 Ultimate Tips You Should Know Before You Start Running!*

**Book 2**: *5K Fury: 10 Proven Steps to Get You to the Finish Line in 9 weeks or less!*

**Book 3:** *10K Titan: Push Beyond the 5K in 6 Weeks or Less!*

**Book 4:** *Beginner's Guide to Half Marathons: A Simple Step-By-Step Solution to Get You to the Finish Line in 12 Weeks!*

**Book 5:** *Long Run Hacks: 20 Ultimate Tips to Help You Push Through Hard Runs!*

### Coming Soon:

**Book 6:** *Marathon Machine - Breakthrough Your Running Barrier and Conquer Your Dream!*

Long Run Hacks

## About the Author

I played sports throughout my youth and even into my adult years. I ran my first 5k at the age of 37 in March of 2008 without any training at all. I finished in third place, although my leg muscles felt like I deserved first place. My legs were sore for six days after the race. My next 5k attempt was in 2015 at the age of 42 in my local hometown. I had no intention of placing at all. I ended up running worse than my first 5k by almost two minutes. I placed second with no training at all. I thought I would have learned a lesson by now - nope.

In May 2016, I was flying to Las Vegas for our yearly guys' trip. I was reading a *Sky Mall* magazine, and I came across an article called "Top 100 things to do in Las Vegas." Number eight on the list was run a race through the streets of Las Vegas. During the race, the city blocks off sections of the strip. I was hooked. They offered a 5k, 10k, half marathon and marathon. I liked walking a lot; in fact, one of my favorite things to do in Las Vegas was to see how many steps I could get in a day (my record to date is 42,000). The Rock-and-Roll Half Marathon/Marathon would be taking place in November 2016. I scoured the Internet for any information related to training for a half marathon.

My wife asked me, "Why in the world do you want to run a half marathon?" I told her because I was physically able to. She said, "You just want to put one of those 13.1 stickers on the back of your car." But truthfully the real reason was much deeper than that. Whenever I catch a fresh dump of powder on my snowboard, there is no other experience like it. I feel like a kid again, and I feel alive. The real reason I wanted to run was that I wanted to feel the accomplishment, feel the pain and feel the glory of crossing the finish line all the while feeling alive. Running allows me to unleash that competitive kid inside me who yearns to feel alive.